# The Adventures of Scuba Jack

The Adventures of Scuba Jack

Narwhal, walrus, dolphin and seal.
Blue Whale, sea horse, shark and eel.
All these creatures swim wild and free.
LITTLE FISH,
swim the oceans with me.

A **PoLaR BEaR**
eats fish and seals.
He's not picky when it comes to his meals.

A Black Tip **SHARK** has teeth so white.
He darts away til he's out of sight.

Narwhal and Beluga **WHaLES**
are out searching for lunch.
A school of minnows is hiding, clustered in a bunch.

The largest creature is the big, Blue Whale.

He's **100 FEET** long from head to his tai

# THE ATLANTIC SAILFISH

is so fast.
He leaps from the water with a powerful blast.

Gentoo **Penguins**
cannot fly, but love to swim.
They waddle to the water and dive right in.

# WALRUSES use their tusks to haul themselves out of water onto the ice.

They also use their tusks to defend themselves from predators. Isn't that nice?

A father SEA HORSE
cares for his babies and keeps them well.
In his pouch is where they love to dwell.

# DOLPHINS

swim beside a tuna school.
They offer protection
from sharks, isn't that cool?

Now my suit and flippers are squeaky clean.
Even my cute little submarine.
My bubbly bathtub is a fun place to be.
Oh, I do love exploring the beautiful

Sea.

# How Many Animals?

Sharks ☐  Polar Bears ☐  Walruses ☐  Sailfish ☐

Gentoo Penguins ☐  Beluga Whales ☐  Seahorses ☐

# Decode the Message

| | |
|---|---|
| A | 1 |
| B | 2 |
| C | 3 |
| D | 4 |
| E | 5 |
| F | 6 |
| G | 7 |
| H | 8 |
| I | 9 |
| J | 10 |
| K | 11 |
| L | 12 |
| M | 13 |
| N | 14 |
| O | 15 |
| P | 16 |
| Q | 17 |
| R | 18 |
| S | 19 |
| T | 20 |
| U | 21 |
| V | 22 |
| W | 23 |
| X | 24 |
| Y | 25 |
| Z | 26 |

_ _ _ _ _   _ _ _ _ _ ,   _ _ _ _ _

19 3 21 2 1   10 1 3 11 19   8 15 21 19 5